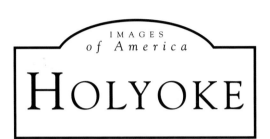

IMAGES
of America

HOLYOKE

Dedicated to all the people of Holyoke,
both near and far.

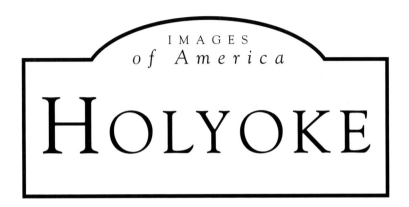

IMAGES
of America

HOLYOKE

Craig P. Della Penna

ARCADIA

ISBN 0-7524-0582-9

Published by Arcadia Publishing,
an imprint of the Chalford Publishing Corporation,
One Washington Center, Dover, New Hampshire 03820.
Printed in Great Britain

Library of Congress Cataloging-in-Publication Data applied for

Contents

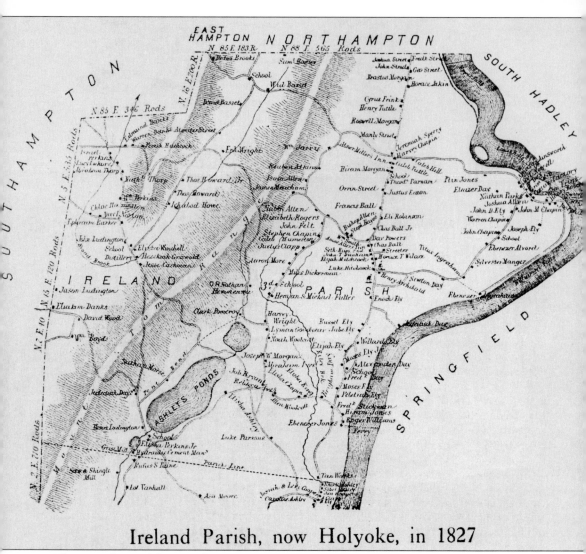

Ireland Parish, now Holyoke, in 1827

The main thoroughfare seen here is today known as Northampton Street. At this time, Ireland Parish was a part of West Springfield and interestingly enough, had few if any people of Irish descent. It is one of Holyoke's biggest ironies that when mostly populated with people from England, Holyoke had an Irish name, and later when it had a substantial Irish population, it acquired the English name of today. (From the collection of the Holyoke Public Library.)

Introduction

The city of Holyoke is located in Hampden County and is surrounded by the communities of Chicopee, South Hadley, Westfield, Southampton, and Easthampton. Holyoke was established as a town in 1850, incorporated as a city in 1873, and occupies a land area of 21.2 square miles.

Holyoke was the first planned industrial community in the United States. Boston industrialists, recognizing the potential of the 50-foot drop in the Connecticut River at South Hadley Falls, constructed what was at the time the largest dam in the world. Their company—Hadley Falls Company, a direct forerunner of today's Holyoke Water Power Company—then laid out a community ideally suited to manufacturing and commercial enterprise. Four and a half miles of canals were dug by picks and shovels through the lower wards, and all types of products were manufactured along their banks. Paper grew as the dominant force in the city, and at one time, over twenty-five paper mills were in operation.

Within thirty years, Holyoke was recognized by the nation as "The Queen of Industrial Cities" and "The Paper City of the World." As Holyoke matured, it began to diversify industrially. Steam pumps, blank books, silk goods, hydrants, bicycles, and trolleys were among a growing list of goods being shipped all over the world. Today, Holyoke is a fully diversified industrial city. Many of the old mills are occupied by a full range of manufacturing enterprises, large and small. And in the typically New England version of recycling, the rest of the 150-year-old mills now host hi-tech service enterprises.

Holyoke Public Library, a center for all informational needs: educational, recreational, cultural, research, reference, and referrals, has been serving the region since 1870. In its magnificent Greek-revival building, the library organizes, preserves, and makes freely available printed and non-printed materials to anyone interested in the pursuit of education, information, and to anyone interested in a creative use of leisure time.

The Holyoke Public Library is pleased to add Images of Holyoke to its Holyoke History collection. This is a book that speaks not only from one person to another, and from one culture to another, but from one generation, and one age, to another. This book provides the union of understanding that links the generations, makes it possible to share human experience down through time. We are honored to have played a part providing some of the included photos.

The library seeks to promote endeavors which will stimulate and expand the reading interest of both children and adults and to coordinate this work with that of other educational, social, and cultural groups in the community. It is largely staffed by volunteers and encourages those inclined to join this group that enriches Holyoke while being enriched themselves.

There are many rewards when working in a library. One of the great rewards is gaining a close glimpse into history and thereby learning about the community through its collection and its people. We extend an invitation to the readers to visit the Holyoke Public Library and its History Room.

Maria Pagan and Paul Graves,
Holyoke Public Library

Preface

If you grew up in the 1960s or earlier and you said that you were from Holyoke, well . . . that was a name that conjured-up many positive images. High quality paper and other manufactured goods were the first thoughts that came to mind. You were shown respect, as being from Holyoke was synonymous with having a good work ethic. It was known the world over that being brought-up in Holyoke meant that you were exposed to a cross-section of people from many economic and ethnic/cultural origins. It also meant that you were brought up in a community that was tolerant and you could fit in anywhere.

Somehow that positive image changed in the 1970s. I suppose it had to do with the frequent and horrendous fires of those years, as well as the changing marketplace that caused nearly all the paper mills to move away, taking with them many of the good-paying manufacturing jobs. It always pained me to see my hometown as having a tarnished reputation. There is so much positive about Holyoke and its people that I felt it was not being given a fair shake.

In the spring of 1996, I was at a bookstore in Keene, New Hampshire, and came upon a book by Alan Rumrill called *Images of Keene*, published by Arcadia Publishing. It was unusual with its sepia-toned cover that caught your eye. As you perused it, you discovered it was all archive pictures with short captions. I thought, what a great idea!! A book to pique your interest in local history. I was doing a series of slide lectures on the railroad history of the area, and I thought it might be nice to learn a little more of the city of Keene so I bought the book.

Later that fall, while at a book publishers convention in Boston, I came upon the booth of the Arcadia Publishing Company and was astonished to learn that they are in essence doing the whole country with these haunting, yet interesting books. I asked if they had enlisted anyone to do my home town of Holyoke.

I spent the winter of 96–97 gathering these unforgettable pictures and talking with some of Holyoke's most respected historians. I was stunned by the texture and feeling of these images. I think that you too, will be surprised by what you are about to see. Your eyes are about to be opened, and you will never look at Holyoke in the same way again.

The book that follows was not done by a professional historian who is intimately in tune with the minute details of this grand old city; instead, it was done by a native Holyoker (HHS graduate, class of '70), who wants everyone to see that the city by the dam, is truly one of America's most intriguing cities.

Craig P. Della Penna

One

The "Plan"

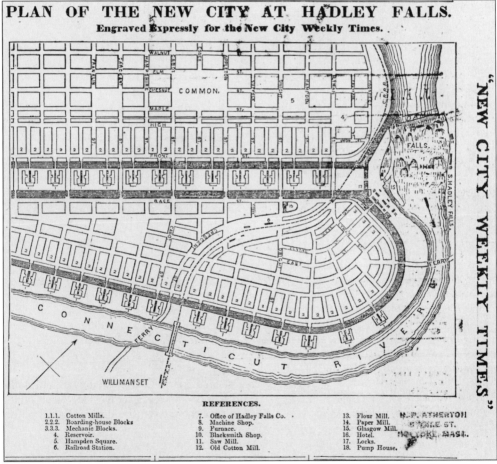

PLAN OF THE NEW CITY AT HADLEY FALLS.

Engraved Expressly for the New City Weekly Times.

"NEW CITY WEEKLY TIMES"

COMMON.

FALLS.

CONNECTICUT RIVER

WILLIMANSET

REFERENCES.

1.1.1. Cotton Mills.	7. Office of Hadley Falls Co.	13. Flour Mill.
2.2.2. Boarding-house Blocks	8. Machine Shop.	14. Paper Mill.
3.3.3. Mechanic Blocks.	9. Furnace.	15. Glasgow Mill.
4. Reservoir.	10. Blacksmith Shop.	16. Hotel.
5. Hampden Square.	11. Saw Mill.	17. Locks.
6. Railroad Station.	12. Old Cotton Mill.	18. Pump House.

The planned community known as "New City" was the creation of the Hadley Falls Company, which was formed on April 28, 1848. The Massachusetts Legislature created the corporation, whose purpose was to develop the natural power of the Hadley Falls for manufacturing. This engraving was introduced to the public in 1849 and was the basis for the development of the city. "The Plan" was still in effect when the last section of canal was dug about forty years later. The unique idea to use the height of the falls to create a network of canals for power was the vision of one man, George Ewing. (From the collection of the Holyoke Public Library.)

George C. Ewing came to the area in 1846 as the sales representative of the Fairbanks Scale Company of St. Johnsbury, Vermont. He was impressed with the falls and in the terraced and sloping geology on the western side of the river. He convinced his superiors in the great need for a dam in this location, and they gave him the authority to purchase large tracts of land from the farmers of the area. He was quiet as to his purpose so he would not antagonize the locals and drive up the price. He was successful in the quest for land, and the Fairbanks Company sold the idea and their holdings to interests in the Boston area who formed the Hadley Falls Company. (From the collection of the Holyoke Public Library.)

The Connecticut River before the construction of the dam was home to a vibrant fishing industry. Salmon and shad both returning from the ocean in the spring of each year were so plentiful that the Native American tribes of past years said the water turned black from their numbers. In this engraving from picturesque Hamden in 1892, it shows commercial fisherman plying the waters at night near Jed Day's Landing, a ferry that was based in the Springdale neighborhood. (From the collection of John Doherty.)

Construction of the first dam was started in 1847. On November 16, 1848, at 10:00 am, the gates were closed, and the reservoir behind it began to rise. Almost immediately the dam began to leak. At 3:26 that afternoon, the dam was swept away. John Chase, the local agent in charge of construction, telegraphed Boston with the now famous message, "Dam gone to hell by way of Willimansett." The decision was made right away to rebuild with a stronger wooden dam and then as soon as possible build a stone dam. This early view shows the dam without the apron, which was added in 1870 to alleviate the deterioration at the base from the years of pounding water. (From the archives of the Holyoke Water Power Company.)

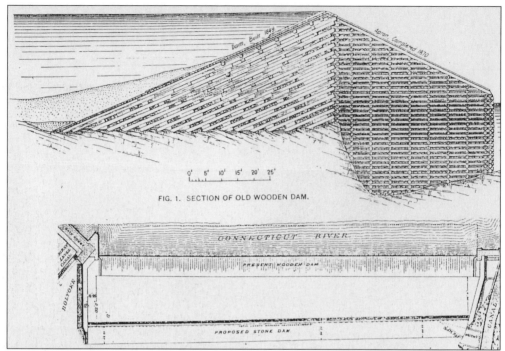

FIG. 1. SECTION OF OLD WOODEN DAM.

These architectural drawings of the dam show the cross section of the wooden dam and its interesting sloping arrangement. Remnants of this old dam are still in place behind the stone dam, and in times of high water, it causes a ripple effect that can be seen from above. (From the archives of the Holyoke Water Power Company.)

This interesting view taken in about the mid-1880s shows the original gatehouse to the canal system in great detail. The walkway is on a dam that separates the canal head-waters from the river. On the day of this picture, the canal is dry, probably for maintenance reasons. Note the single arch to the left of the gatehouse. (From the archives of the Holyoke Water Power Company.)

This is a rare view of the aqueduct coming off of the gatehouse in the 1860s. The aqueduct carried water that was pumped from the river at the gatehouse and transported across the Connecticut River Railroad right-of-way and then into a reservoir that used to be located at the end of High Street near Lyman Street The reservoir was filled-in during 1871. (From the archives of the Holyoke Water Power Company.)

This circular from the era of about 1875 is a marketing blurb that details the positive benefits of siting your manufacturing or commercial establishment in the new city of Holyoke. Holyoke Water Power Company (HWP), successor of the Hadley Falls Company, was the real estate company, power source, and the major player in the politics of early Holyoke. Some might call HWP's place in the development of Holyoke as one of a beneficial monarchy that doled out parcels to enterprises that would provide for the economic diversity and enhancement of the community. (From the archives of Holyoke Water Power Company.)

This view from 1893 shows a group of folks on a Sunday, biking and walking at the headwaters of the first level canal. The apron on the wooden dam is clearly visible, as well as the early construction of the stone dam. The straight trench, about 150 feet in front of the existing dam, shows the location of the future stone dam. The overhead cables that reach to the tower on the far side will be used to bring and position the stones on the new dam. (From the collection at the Holyoke Heritage State Park.)

The tailings pile, or waste pile, for the excavation of the footing for the stone dam is evident here in this picture. Note the relatively new County Bridge here in 1893 (torn down in 1995). Also, the clear view, one without brush and sumac trees, from Prospect Park, now known as Pulaski Park, is something to be envious of. (From the archives of Holyoke Water Power Company.)

In 1893, the investors/executives of HWP are seen here checking out the early construction work on the stone dam. Note the flimsy trestle work for the work trains that will transport out the waste ledge. (From the archives of Holyoke Water Power Company.)

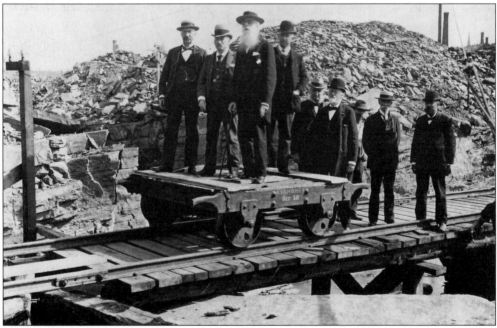

The eyes of the world's engineering community were on Holyoke because this project was constructing the longest dam in the world. Over 1,000 feet long and 30 feet high, it was going to be a crowning achievement for these executives. In this close-up view of the tailings piles, one can see how much ledge was excavated for the footing of the dam. (From Wistariahurst Museum.)

With the wooden dam and the Holyoke skyline for a back-drop, the new dam began to be constructed by the Holyoke Water Power Company. In this picture (on the right) is a clear view of the suspended cable which transported both men and materials. (From Wistariahurst Museum.)

Like a giant jigsaw puzzle, all the granite blocks that make up the Holyoke Dam were milled with precision and numbered so the workmen knew where each block went. They came from the extensive quarry operation at Vinalhaven, Maine, and were transported by barge and then finally by rail to the storage yard near the dam. (From the archives of the Holyoke Water Power Company.)

The enormity of the project is apparent in this photograph. Massive granite blocks were anchored to the river bedrock and faced with angled stones to use the weight of the water for an advantage to strengthen the structure. Note the elaborate jib cranes and steam engine. (From Wistariahurst Museum.)

In this 1899 photograph, the project nears completion. Note the size of the workers. (From the archives of the Holyoke Water Power Company.)

Now the last part of the "plan," a permanent dam, is complete with the laying of the last stone on the cold day of January 4, 1900. The intricacies of the nearly lost art of stone masonry can be easily seen here in this picture. The vast majority of the laborers used in the construction of both the dam and the canals were Irish. For their labors they were paid about 75¢ a day. During the construction of the first (failed) wooden dam, the work force went on strike. Protesting the lack of a wanted 5¢ an hour raise and forced to work on Sundays, the strikers went back only after the militia was called in and they were consoled by a local priest. (From Wistariahurst Museum.)

When seen from the South Hadley side on this day, the dry dam contains the ghostly quiet and still Connecticut River. Note the few men on the apron of the dam who I believe are not workers, but only folks out for a stroll. (From the collection at the Holyoke Heritage State Park.)

This scene from the 1940s shows the South Hadley side and an unusual concrete structure that is an unsuccessful fish ladder. By this time, the once abundant shad and salmon were virtually extinct above the dam, and this system was tried to get them upstream. On May 23, 1955, a new type of mechanical lift went into operation. Much like an elevator, the new lift was a success that was emulated all over the country and allowed for today's replenished game fish stocks. (From the archives of the Holyoke Water Power Company.)

The freshet of 1894 interfered with the construction of the new stone dam. The cranes in the river are forced to wait for drier times to resume their work. The high water here, though impressive, was not noteworthy. The old New Haven Railroad 36-foot wooden box cars carried tools and material to the job site. (From the archives of the Holyoke Water Power Company.)

The flood of 1927 was the highest in recorded history (up till then). At 14.75 feet above the dam, the flood was somewhat unexpected, coming as it did in November after heavy rains. It was necessary to sandbag the railroad tracks as the river threatened to go over them, around the gatehouse, and then into the canal system uncontrolled. This certainly would have destroyed many of the mills and made for a much larger disaster. (From the archives of the Holyoke Water Power Company.)

In 1853, the canals began to be dug by hand, with ox- and horse-drawn wagons moving the loosened earth. In 1859, the first steam excavator came on-line to speed up the work. The final sections of the third level canal were not finished until the late 1800s. (From the collection of John Doherty.)

The waters of the canal system, after passing through most mills to develop power, eventually empty into the river. A gatehouse controls the level here at Number 4, which is near today's Sonoco Plant at the foot of Sargeant Street on the third level canal. (From the archives of Holyoke Water Power Company.)

Here is a rich textured scene from approximately 1890. The canal is drained for the maintenance of the wall which has suffered a small collapse here. This is on the second level canal where the junction of Race and Main Streets are. The large building above the workmen is the famous Flat-Iron Building. Just up the street is the old post office building, and on the far right is the trolley shelter on the corner of Dwight and Race Streets. I remember having breakfast there many times in the 1970s when it was a small restaurant. I did not know that it used to be a trolley station until I started to do this project. (From the archives of the Holyoke Water Power Company.)

A view of the same general area from a further distance back shows the light duty bridges that used to be the standard design. The arched steel bridge over the canal is of course Lyman Street Bridge, and the covered bridge on the left is the Connecticut River Railroad Bridge with the passenger station just barely visible behind it. Note the advertising under the railroad bridge and the rowboat in the canal. (From the collection at the Holyoke Heritage State Park.)

The 1950s aerial image shows the dam and upper canal area, which were the integral parts of the "plan" carried out by HWP to develop the city. The major changes in this view from today's status are at the top, between Pulaski Park and Lyman Street. This is the neighborhood that was the target of urban renewal in the 1960s. Virtually all of this old Polish section has been renovated. (From the archives of the Holyoke Water Power Company.)

In the 1920s, a company out of New York, known as the Fairchild Company and under contract to HWP, took a number of aerial photos of the city. This one shows a circular building along the river which is the old Gas Works of the Holyoke Gas & Electric Company. Here they converted coal to synthetic gas used for cooking and heating. Interestingly, the waste from this operation is attracting attention today due the discovery of coal tar in the river adjacent to where the plant stood. This will be cleaned up in 1998–1999. (From the archives of the Holyoke Water Power.)

Here is the headquarters of the Holyoke Water Power Company. The mansard-roofed and ivy-covered structure has been a part of this community for over a hundred years. The building in the right background is the old Boston & Maine (B & M) passenger station, and on the left is the Mt. Tom Hose Company, better known as the fire station. (From the archives of the Holyoke Water Power Company.)

In the early 1950s, the management of HWP sought to develop the last in-town parcel of industrial potential. Located in the Springdale section, it furthered their "plan" for Holyoke by helping small businesses locate and build here. Some incentives were brought out in terms of land development and utility infrastructure enhancements. Soon a number of quality and reputable manufacturers sprang up in the area. This sign at the entrance to the park featured "Reddy Kilowatt," an icon of the 1950s seen everywhere, including television commercials. (From the archives of the Holyoke Water Power Company.)

Here, under construction in 1956, is the Acme Chain Corporation. This plant is still here and actually expanded in 1996. The residential neighborhood of Springdale is in the foreground, and on the right side is the three-story building that housed Reynolds Paper. A major player in the paper converting industry, Reynolds was known the world over for its line of paper products. Today, it is the home of RUWAC Industrial Vacuums and Railroad Distribution Services, the area's premier, intermodal distribution facility. (From the archives of the Holyoke Water Power Company.)

This shows the area of Springdale in the 1940s and gives a good representation of the large tract that became the industrial park. The ball field on the bottom is Springdale Park, which was designed by the nationally known landscape architect, Frederick Olmstead, before the turn of the century. Interestingly, Olmstead was the first noted proponent of the linear park concept, known today as a "greenway." (From the archives of the Holyoke Water Power Company.)

This view shows the industrial park nearly completed in 1957. The last major site, not developed by this time, was the Rexhall Chemical Company (BASF today). It is situated behind the Reynolds Building, on the curve of Main Street. Both of these aerial shots show the layout of the canals in an interesting way. (From the archives of the Holyoke Water Power Company.)

Two
Industry

This view looking north from the Sargeant Street Bridge over the first level canal was taken in the 1930s. It shows an active, well-maintained city, full of opportunity and hope for residents. This sort of a working-smokestack-view of the world was typically shown to represent an all-is-well slant on things. Interestingly, a similar view of this particular scene can be had every day by simply driving into Holyoke by way of I-391. (From the archives of the Holyoke Water Power Company.)

In the 1880s, J.W. Jolley Company had a thriving business on Bridge and Crescents Streets. They did contract machine shop work for the large mills in town and were a viable business until the 1980s, when they were bought out by the Central Mass Machine Shop Company, which is still prospering in this structure. (From the collection at the Holyoke Heritage State Park.)

One of the big-name paper mills in Holyoke during the 1930s was the American Writing Paper Company, Riverside Division. Makers of the fine Eagle A Writing Paper and located along the third level canal at Cabot Street, they were later to become the National Blank Book Company. The canal is emptied here for maintenance and shows how the water goes through the gate area into the mill. The curved railroad bridge leads to the right into the Boston & Maine Railroad yard behind Crescent Street. (From the archives of the Holyoke Water Power Company.)

The Holyoke Water Power Company's standard contract with the mills sited along the canals had a provision allowing HWP to be paid in silver for units of "Millpower" (a term of measurement of the hydraulic power that passes through a mill complex). This was the so-called "Silver Clause," and in essence, it said that for each Millpower granted, the yearly rent of 260 ounces of Troy weight of silver would be paid. It was not too often they were paid in that fashion; though in the 1930s, American Writing Paper Company did. Here a Railway Express Agency truck is shown delivering the bars of pure silver to HWP. (From the archives of the Holyoke Water Power Company.)

Time Table of the Holyoke Mills

TO TAKE EFFECT ON AND AFTER JAN. 3d, 1853

*The standard being that of the Western Rail Road,
which is the Meridian time at Cambridge*

MORNING BELLS
First Bell ring at 4.40, A.M.   Second Bell ring in
at 5, A.M.

YARD GATES
Will be opened at ringing of Morning Bells, of Meal
Bells, and of Evening Bells, and kept open ten
minutes.

WORK COMMENCES
At ten minutes after last Morning Bell, and ten minutes after Bell which "rings in" from Meals.

BREAKFAST BELLS
October 1st, to March 31st, inclusive, ring out at
7 A.M., ring in at 7:30 A.M.

April 1st to Sept. 30th, inclusive, ring out at 6:30
A.M., ring in at 7 A.M.

DINNER BELLS
Ring out at 12:30 P.M., ring in at 1 P.M.

EVENING BELLS
Ring out at 6.30†, P.M.

†Excepting on Saturdays when the Sun sets previous to 6:30.   At such times, ring out
at Sunset.
In all cases, the *first* stroke of the Bell is considered as marking the time.

This handout from 1853 shows the schedule for the six-day work week. You had better not be late either. (From the collection of the Holyoke Public Library.)

The 1891 weekday lunch crowd is going back to work, and most of them are women. This was the Thread Mill along the third level canal. (From the collection of John Doherty.)

This view of the Thread Mill is from the other direction and taken around 1900. It shows clearly the layout of the structures along Canal Street to the right and the curve of the third level canal at the Valley Paper Company in the background. The old Thread Mill Building became Graham Medical Products in more recent years, and Graham Medical Products closed in 1995. (From the collection at Holyoke Heritage State Park.)

A closer view of the Valley Paper Company is shown here. Taken at the turn of the century, it clearly shows the hip-roofed office nearest the bridge and the unusually grand slate roof with the name of the company done in contrasting slate. Valley Paper came to Holyoke in 1866, and this structure still stands as the home for the city's elder care services. (From the collection at the Holyoke Heritage State Park.)

This is looking south along the second level canal where Cabot Street crosses over the bridge at Race Street. The large mill is actually called the Holyoke Water Power Company Mill. This was a forerunner of the "incubator" concept that community developers and planners of today talk about. Here's how it worked: HWP would lease space to your small start-up company, and you could grow as you needed and also take advantage of the economics of scale because you were one of many companies within the complex. For example, it was more cost effective to share certain common areas such as shipping and receiving, heating, and power. (From the archives of the Holyoke Water Power Company.)

Here is the other mill of the Riverside Paper Company along the third level canal. Interestingly, the Hadley Falls Company envisioned Holyoke as a textile city, and they opposed efforts to establish paper mills. That was until Parsons Paper came to town in 1853, shortly after the dam was built. Parsons was an instant success and paved the way for others to arrive. By 1891, there were nineteen other paper mills, a pulp mill, and five paper converters operating in Holyoke, and the city became known as the "Paper City of the World." (From the collection at the Holyoke Heritage State Park.)

In 1865, the Merrick Thread was completed. This complex employed about five hundred people who made threads and yarn. Merrick was among the first major companies in town, and this view shows it along Appleton Street at the first level canal. This complex stood near Heritage Park, until it burned in 1994. (From the collection at the Holyoke Heritage State Park.)

This photograph, looking east, was taken from the city hall around 1890. The Willard Lumber Company was a customer of the Holyoke & Westfield Railroad, a unit of the New Haven Railroad. The three mill buildings are known as the Lyman Mills, and they, along with Parsons Paper, were among the first in town in 1854. Interestingly, these mills were some of the few mill complexes that were actually built to take full advantage of the full difference in the water level between the canals. The domed structure in the foreground is the famed Opera House, burned down in 1967, and just to the right is the Windsor Hotel, which burned around 1930. (From the collection at the Holyoke Heritage State Park.)

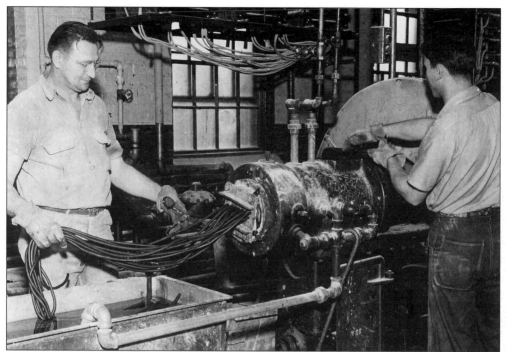

Holyoke used to have unusual industries in addition to paper and textiles. For example, in 1945, one of the smaller concerns was Paul Martin Rubber Company, which extruded rubber into round strips. Here two workers are feeding raw material and cutting the finished stock. This company is still in business today. (From the archives of the Holyoke Water Power Company.)

The Skinner Mill complex stood where Heritage Park is today. It is ironic that this great enterprise, a silk mill, became the singular corporate symbol of Holyoke, the paper city. William Skinner brought his business to Holyoke after a flood destroyed his original complex in Williamsburg. HWP provided a lot of financial incentives, free land, free power, and reduced interest rate construction loans, to convince Skinner that Holyoke was the place to relocate his business. It was a good investment for HWP because this was the major employer in town for almost one hundred years. (From the collection at the Holyoke Heritage State Park.)

In 1871, Joseph Curtis Lewis arrived from Maine and constructed the lumber mill that stood along the cove in the river just above the dam. This was the first large mill that was this close to a large population, and it was immensely successful. Most of the wooden houses in Holyoke were framed with material from this complex, and the Connecticut River Railroad shipped many cars of finished lumber to points east and south. (From the collection of the Highland Hardware & Bike Shop.)

For quite a few years, huge log drives were using the river as a highway. Employing upwards of four hundred men and stretching for almost 100 miles in length, this was an impressive site. It is interesting to note that in most cases the men were not paid until they reached Holyoke, where a number of saloons awaited the rowdy and thirsty customers. The Holyoke Police Department used to dread the arrival of the log drives. (From the collection of John Doherty.)

Here is good view of the cove and the scope and size of the complex. A good job for boys was to collect and sell kindling wood which was waste to the lumber company. (From the collection of John Doherty.)

You were one of the lucky few if you had a goat to pull the cart. Note the size of the pile from which they're working. (From the collection of John Doherty.)

William B. Whiting Coal Company was one of the first full service fuel dealers in town providing coal and wood. The store-front office was located on Dwight Street just below the city hall. This view shows the large coal storage facility that used to be nearby. This photograph was done for some advertising, and the large structure was not really visible in this fashion. It should be noted that they are still in business, successful, and located on Lyman Street. (From the collection at the Holyoke Heritage State Park.)

Three
Commercial

A city's economic heart is where the commercial district lies. Holyoke is unusual in that it has had three distinct and different locations for the heart of the commerce in town. Of course, today's center is the Holyoke Mall. The area that preceded until around 1970 was High Street or downtown. What not many people realize is that the first commercial district in the city was the area of Dwight and Main Streets. This was known as Depot Square, and it was adjacent to the railroad freight yards and only one block from the passenger station. This image from the mid-1880s looks up the Dwight Street hill towards city hall. The street is cobblestoned and has the trolley tracks in place. Note the omnibus on the left and the yeast delivery wagon behind it. (From the collection of the Highland Hardware and Bike Shop.)

This six-panel photograph taken in 1933 shows the Depot Square area on a quiet Sunday morning. A number of interesting components of this picture are worth describing. On the extreme left is the Hotel Jess, which is one of several hotels in this area serving the passengers who arrived at the nearby train station. The covered staircase allows pedestrians to get to the Flats and safely across the tracks. There is an old-style gas station with a tile roof, and just to the left is the freight transfer building of the B & M Railroad. Panning to the right, we see the cobblestoned Main Street with the trolley tracks and the row of stores. This area of Main Street all the way out to Sargeant Street was home to six furniture stores at one time and was "The" place in the Valley to come shopping for furniture. Main Street was truly the main street for most of Holyoke's organized existence. The Hotel Hamilton is on the right side of Dwight Street and rents some ground floor space to the Mechanics Savings Bank. The financial institution in later years became Community Savings Bank, which most recently was absorbed into the Fleet Bank group. Today, the building itself is called the Silvio Conte Training Center. The job training center is named after the well-loved congressman. At the extreme right, a light-colored building is visible; it is the old post office near the intersection of Race Street. It should be noted that Race Street is not thus named in competition senses, but instead refers to the race-way of the adjacent second level canal.

In addition to the businesses visible in this series of images, the Main Street area was home to many neighborhood type businesses. These *mom & pop* stores catered to all the ethnic types

that were nearby. A French bakery, a Jewish meat market, a German wurst shop, and an Irish grocery were typical examples of local places. About six blocks south of here stood the Dreikorn Bakery. My grandfather was employed by Dreikhorn's as a delivery truck driver during this era, and he was always grateful that he had a job during the Depression. Near to Dreikhorn's was the Turn Verin Club on Bridge Street. This was formed by a German community so that they could exercise on Sundays. Massachusetts "Blue Laws" forbid some outdoor activities on Sundays unless sponsored by clubs of this sort.

A pou-pourri of businesses could also be found near Depot Square. For example, some of these concerns were Chase & Coolidge, a supplier of industrial components (still in business); a veterinarian by the name of T.J. Shinkin, which was inside the Hotel Monat at 4 Main Street; Quirk Paper at 30 Main Street; Marcus Printing at 32 Main Street (still in business at the other end of Main Street); Holyoke News & Leather Goods at 87 Main Street; H.E. Taylor Produce Company at 93 Main Street; Hotel Lawler, located at 77 Main Street; J.B. Glenny Furnished Rooms at 151 Main Street; and on and on.

One could even be entertained in this area as well. The Bijou and the Majestic playing the latest in first-run movies were the old-style theaters with plush seating and balconies that overlooked the stage. By the way, the two police officers are actually only one, a John White, who got into the first and last shots. (From the collection of the Highland Hardware and Bike Shop.)

That staircase from the previous view is seen here again in an earlier version with an abundance of children filling the photographer's lens. This view from 1891 shows two of the new electric trolleys in service, with one on Main Street and the other making its way down Dwight Street. (From the collection of John Doherty.)

This view from 1867 features the famous Holyoke House. As the premier hotel and only one block from the Connecticut River Railroad passenger station, it was host to many important people. This structure is still here today, but the top two floors have been removed. Now, it is the Silvio Conte Training Center. (From the collection of John Doherty.)

This view comes from an advertisement from the 1870s and shows the structure as owned by Mr. E.M. Belden. Note the quick connection to the train station. Built in 1850, the year of Holyoke's incorporation as a town, the Holyoke House Hotel rivaled the best that were available in Boston. (From the collection of the Holyoke Public Library.)

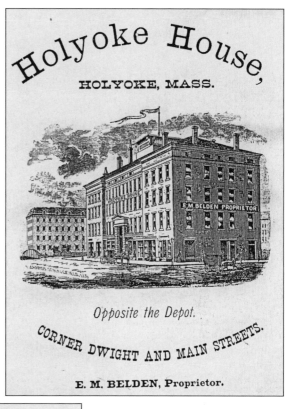

Holyoke House,

HOLYOKE, MASS.

Opposite the Depot.

CORNER DWIGHT AND MAIN STREETS.

E. M. BELDEN, Proprietor.

This is a photograph of High and Appleton Streets in the early spring of 1960. This structure is one of the more interesting commercial buildings in town. The Parkwest Bank on the first floor is still there today. Note the shamrock painted in the intersection. This was for the big St. Patrick's Day Parade which passed by here every year. (From the collection of the John Woods Real Estate Company.)

45

The Naumkeag Clothing Company on High Street was a popular place at the turn of the century. This advertisement from that era shows the well-lit store with its many windows and abundance of clothes. The building is no longer standing. (From the collection at the Holyoke Heritage State Park.)

The Holyoke Machine Company had their offices located here on the second floor of the 400 block of Main Street at Sargeant Street. On the ground floor were a few commercial enterprises, like the Curran Bros. Paint Company, which also sold "Cold Soda." (From the collection of the Holyoke Public Library.)

The Flat-Iron Building was one of Holyoke's most architecturally interesting buildings. Located at the junction of Main and Race Streets, it served as the offices of American Writing Paper Company. This early 1890s view shows the electrified trolley tracks in place and some activity going on in the morning. (From the collection of the Holyoke Public Library.)

This close-up view of the Flat-Iron was taken later in the 1890s. One of the changes included a fire hydrant, and also Bardwell's Drug Store & Barber Shop occupied some of the retail space. The Flat-Iron was torn down in 1960, and this area is now the site of a former Shawmut Bank branch. (From the collection of the Holyoke Public Library.)

In the early 1930s, Homer Rainault bought the old Bridge Street gas works from the city and converted it to an arena. Called the Valley Arena, it hosted many a night of big-name prizefighters, such as Rocky Marciano, Willie Pep, and Jack Dempsey, who was a referee here in his later years. On nights without a prizefight, the arena became a dance floor, and you could expect to see Tommy Dorsey, Vaughan Monroe, Lionel Hampton, and Lawrence Welk. The seating capacity was four thousand, and there was never a disturbance or problem here. It burned down in the early 1960s, and today it is the site of a small park. (From the collection of the Holyoke Public Library.)

Maple and Appleton Streets are seen here in this late 1890s photograph. The building on the right is the old YMCA, which burned in 1943. The large interesting apartment building is the Louis Lafrance Block, which burned in the 1970s. I remember Chester's Drug Store as being the place to meet before the dances which were held at the War Memorial Building across the street. (From the collection at the John Woods Real Estate Company.)

Here on High Street opposite the city hall in the 1920s, we see a cobblestone street and Liggetts Drug Store. The building on the far right is the McAuslin Wakelin Store. The brownstone building was the Osborne Hardware Store, and most recently, it was the Moriarty Law Office. (From the archives of the Holyoke Water Power Company.)

49

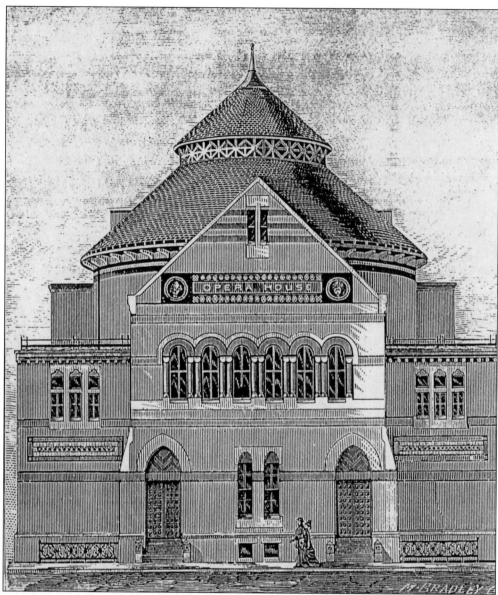

On March 25, 1878, the Opera House opened to a thrilled audience. Built by Mr. Whiting who owned one of the prospering paper mills, this became a landmark in the city. Holyoke was one of the stops for the touring companies out of New York, and some of the greatest of American actors and actresses came to the town . Sarah Bernhardt, George M. Cohan, and Al Jolson all played here, and they praised the acoustics of the building. The structure stood at the corner of Front and John Streets and was attached to the adjacent Windsor Hotel, where you could retire after an evening of theater. It was a smashing success from 1878–1912. In the following years, it underwent a series of owners and formats that met with declining fortunes. In 1948, E.M. Loews bought it and spent $50,000 restoring it for foreign films and second-run features, but that failed also. In 1955, it closed for good, and in 1967, it burned in a spectacular fire.(From the collection of the Holyoke Public Library.)

The Besse Mills Clothing Store stood on the corner of High and Suffolk Streets in the late 1890s. This store specialized in women's clothing. In the second floor windows, they also displayed more of their merchandise. (From the collection of the Holyoke Public Library.)

Holyoke used to have a Walgreen Drug Store located on the corner of Suffolk and High Streets. Here in the 1930s, things look pretty busy for the Depression. (From the collection of the John Woods Real Estate Company.)

This view of High Street, taken in the early 1930s, shows the area that is across the street from today's HAPCO Auto Parts store. Note the Pullman Diner and the billboard advertising new Studebakers for only $645. (From the archives of the Holyoke Water Power Company.)

This image is a view of the opposite side of the street from the upper photograph. It must have been taken a year earlier because the billboard advertising the Studebakers is not there. The large building housing the furniture store is today's HAPCO Building. (From the archive of the Holyoke Water Power Company.)

Holyoke's newspaper, *The Holyoke Transcript*, was located toward the north end of High Street. This view from the 1880s shows the building and some of the employees in the windows. *The Holyoke Transcript* moved to Whiting Farm Road in the 1970s and eventually closed in 1991. The photographs taken by the company photographers are now in Concord, New Hampshire. (From the collection of the Holyoke Public Library.)

In 1907, the McAuslin-Wakelin Building on High Street burned. Holyoke Fire Department is seen here in a mop-up operation. The building just beyond the fire scene is now known as the Bank of Boston Building, while the building on the other side of the street was Delaney Marble Building. (From the archives of the Holyoke Water Power Company.)

Delaney's Marble Building, seen here in the late 1890s, sat at the top of the Dwight Street hill across from the city hall. This impressive structure was built by John Delaney in 1885 and was constructed entirely from marble quarried in the area of Proctor, Vermont. This was the premier hotel in Holyoke until the Nonotuck Hotel (later called the Roger Smith Hotel) was built on Maple Street. In its later years, a number of offices were located on the upper floors, and retail space was leased on the ground floor. Child's Shoes was there for many years, as well as W.T. Grant Company. The building was torn down in 1950 to make room for a larger W.T. Grant department store. The marble from this building was taken away in 195 truck loads to a housing development on Route 116 in South Hadley, where it was used as fill. (From the collection of the Holyoke Public Library.)

The Blizzard of 1888 hit the northeast in mid-March. This was the biggest snow storm to ever hit New England and was talked about for years. This view taken on March 15, 1888, shows only the sidewalk in front of the city hall cleared and High Street virtually impassable to horse carriages. (From the archives of the Holyoke Water Power Company.)

In the late 1880s, upper Hamden Street was still gravel and mud, but the recently built Highland block sported a couple of storefronts, including Marshall's grocery store. Today the structure holds the Highland Hardware and Bike Shop, owned and operated by the Craven family. (From the collection of the Highland Hardware and Bike Shop.)

At the corner of Sargeant and Beech Streets stood the H.P. Hood Creamery. The old Divco milk trucks were loaded here, and the milkmen would deliver the freshest dairy products to homes all over the valley. This view from 1960 shows a small convenience store has rented a space. They would grow into Emily & Jenny's Restaurant, a favorite place for the students of nearby Holyoke High School. (From the collection of the Berrena family.)

The Holyoke Diner stood on Bridge Street in the 1930s. This night scene shows the layout of the complex. Note the tracks that lead to the nearby trolley barn. Today this site is occupied by Amedeo's Restaurant. The one steel diner, that I remember, in Holyoke was the Ross Diner on lower Cabot Street, which has been relocated to Quechee, Vermont. The diner has been restored and is still serving breakfasts to this day. (From the archives of the Holyoke Water Power Company.)

During the 1930s, in the Smith's Ferry section of town, a restaurant in the shape of a zeppelin was owned by Salvator "Toto" Lobello. Toto's was popular with the college crowd and used for banquets and proms. This structure burned in November 1938, but was rebuilt. (From the collection of the Holyoke Public Library.)

Toto's was rebuilt into this Art Deco structure, and it served Mr. Lobello well until 1960, when it too burned down. It is interesting to note that the Food Mart Corporation later owned the option on the land to build a supermarket here. In more recent years, proposals for apartments and condominiums were not approved by the City. (From the collection of the Holyoke Public Library.)

Christmas season in downtown Holyoke was always a bustling time. Here at the city hall, a crowd has gathered one evening for what looks to be a Christmas caroling concert. (From the archives of the Holyoke Water Power Company.)

Thursday night was always bargain or sale night in downtown Holyoke. Here in the 1940s, you can see crowds outside Liggett's and Woolworth's. As John Hickey once said, "These were places that had wooden floors with narrow aisles and many clerks to help you." The buses were the way to get there, and they stopped right at the city hall. (From the collection of the Highland Hardware and Bike Shop.)

Four

Housing

Wistariahurst is the former home of William Skinner and his family. Skinner was a successful businessman who had a textile mill in Williamsburg until a dam collapsed in 1874, destroying the complex. After searching the area for a new site, he finally chose Holyoke. His arrangement with HWP included a mill site on the canal system rent free for five years, and for a dollar, he was able to purchase a city block to situate his home. Skinner's house in Williamsburg, which suffered minor damage from the flood, was dismantled, barged to Holyoke, and reconstructed on its present site. The Skinner family occupied this home until 1959, when Katherine Skinner Kilborne, the youngest child of William, deeded the house to the City of Holyoke for cultural and educational purposes. (From the Wistariahurst Museum.)

One of the last operating farms in Holyoke was Whiting's farm. This farm was situated on Northampton Street, where K-Mart Plaza is now located. The adjoining Whiting's Farm Road, which cut through the middle of the property, was built about 1960, and the farm house and outbuildings were torn down in 1970. (From the collection of the John Woods Real Estate Company.)

In 1882, Richard and John Hildreth built a two-family house at 1864–66 Northampton Street. About a year later, they purchased an adjoining 1-acre lot and hennery. John stayed until his death in 1942. A few years later, Eugene Tamburi bought the house and made it into one of New England's most enduring special places, the Yankee Pedlar Inn. (From the collection of the Holyoke Public Library.)

This was the house of Reuben C. Winchester, the head cashier of the HWP. It stood on the corner of Hampden and Lafayette Streets. Today, this area is now the site of Stop & Shop. (From the archives of Holyoke Water Power Company.)

This view dates from the 1930s and shows a little park with a fountain at the intersection of Willow and Laurel Streets. Note the trolley tracks on Laurel Street. The park is still there today, though the fountain does not function. (From the archives of the Holyoke Water Power Company.)

In South Holyoke, there stood the "Battleship" block. It encompassed the entire city block of Canal, Bridge, Summer, and Jackson Streets. Made of yellow brick and with upscale hardwood trim inside, this block was an exclusive address. Only a small fraction remains standing today, the rest having met the wrecking ball. (From the collection of the Holyoke Public Library.)

In 1927, 81 Bond Street was typical of most of the housing for mill workers in the city. Holyoke was unique in this regard as having the largest collection of this type of housing in western Massachusetts. (From the collection of the Holyoke Public Library.)

This rendition of a tenement on South Summer Street is from a book called *The Run of the Mill* by Steve Dunwell and published by David Godine. This interesting and haunting study in black and white is distinctive in its starkness. Some of these places were quite rich in their interior furnishings. One thing that I remember from growing up in a similar place in Elmwood was that the blocks were well kept and spotless. These were places where everyone knew each other, and if you grew up in one of these, you had twenty other mothers watching to make sure you were safe and out of trouble. (From the collection of the Holyoke Public Library.)

The Fairmont section of town is actually part of Oakdale today. It meant that you could see the Fair Mountain and other parts of the city from its close-to-town vantage point. This view is of Oak Street under construction. Interestingly, this was the first street in Holyoke to be paved with asphalt, so it soon became known as "Tar Alley." (From the collection at the Holyoke Heritage State Park.)

This is the section of town known as Riverside. It is best known as South Holyoke today. The bridge is the railroad bridge to Chicopee. Shown here before the Willimansett Bridge was built, the area was very rural with farmhouses overlooking Chicopee. (From the collection at Holyoke Heritage Park.)

When the Hadley Falls Company started the construction of the dam and the other infrastructure, a group of land speculators from Manchester, New Hampshire, bought large tracts of land about 3/4 miles west of the present city hall. They called it Manchester Grounds. It was only in this century that the name has been changed to the Highlands. (From the collection at Holyoke Heritage State Park.)

From the view looking toward South Hadley in the 1880s from the vantage point of the city hall, the dominant feature is the row houses that were built by Lyman Mills for their workers. Holyoke had a number of different styles and types of this housing. Virtually all of these housing units are gone today and have been replaced with government-built row houses during the 1940s. (From the collection at the Holyoke Heritage State Park.)

An eclectic mix of differing styles of apartment buildings are seen here in 1903 at the southeast corner of Hampshire and Elm Streets. The turreted structure on the corner is the Belvedere. (From the archives of the Holyoke Water Power Company.)

Another popular style for Holyoke homes is the Philadelphia Cottage. There are pockets of these still standing, primarily in the Oakdale and Churchill neighborhoods. One good example is in front of the library. These homes in this particular image were located on Beech Street before the turn of the century. (From the collection of the Holyoke Heritage State Park.)

This home at 123 Lincoln Street was built by Mr. F.W. Doane, owner of the Doane & Williams Lumber Company in Willimansett. Mr. Doane is seen in the carriage coming out of the carriage house, and his family is out front waiting to say good-bye. Note the brand-new freshly laid trolley tracks on the unpaved street. (From the collection of the Holyoke Public Library.)

157 Lincoln Street is seen here when owned by the Rolla Kelton family. Kelton was the owner of a profitable butcher shop in town. I'm not sure if the equestrian is a family member or a passer-by. This image and the previous one are from 1892 and taken by Mr. Milan P. Warner. Warner was a commercial photographer in Holyoke during the 1880s through the 1890s. He was a prolific photographer and published *Picturesque Holyoke*, which presented the city at its high mark in economic power and influence. Warner always tried to get people into his photographs of structures and places, believing people to be important components of a successful image. (From the collection of the Holyoke Public Library.)

This is a 1920s photograph of Homestead Avenue and the Sheehan's Dairy. The area today is the location of the Holyoke Community College. (From the collection of the Holyoke Public Library.)

This is a photograph of Fairmont Square in the 1890s, known today as 248–254 Oak Street. (From the collection of the Holyoke Public Library.)

Built in 1886 for Mr. O'Connor, a clothier, this house still stands on 1093 Dwight Street and is one of the grandest in the city. The O'Connor family owned much of the land in the area at the time, and when a street was put in near the house, their name was given to it. (From the collection of the Holyoke Public Library.)

Another house of the Queen Anne era is at 1109 Dwight Street. This was originally built for Michael Finn, the owner of the Holyoke Coal & Wood Company. Both houses on this page were designed by George P.B. Alderman, who was responsible for many of the more ornate Victorian-styled homes in the Highlands. (From the collection of the Holyoke Public Library.)

This big house was built by Mr. Orrin D. Allyn and is still standing on the corner of Locust and Hampshire Streets. Allyn originally came from the hill towns of Hampshire County and bought much of what is today known as Oakdale. He was a shrewd investor of real estate and was the founder of Allyn & O'Donnell Real Estate Company, which is still in business today. (From the collection of the Holyoke Public Library.)

This view from the 1930s shows the house at 34 Columbus Avenue with the resident on the porch tolerating the photographer. (From the collection of the Holyoke Public Library.)

From 1886–1916, Holyoke had another kind of entrepreneur in Carrie Pratt (third from left), who ran a brothel on Lower Westfield Road. Perhaps you've heard the phrase, "Busier than Carrie Pratt on a Saturday night," now you now where it came from. (From the archives of the Holyoke Public Library.)

This was the second parsonage for the Baptist church at South and Northampton Streets. Built in 1881 on the site of the first parsonage, it was converted into a two-family house by the Zwisler Building Contractor Company in 1927. (From the collection of the Holyoke Public Library.)

Three bicyclists are seen here on Northampton Street in 1894, and the photographer has thoughtfully included the Kenilworth Castle, which was under construction at the time. Kenilworth was located near Mountain Park and owned by E.C. Taft, owner of the Albion Paper Co. This was only supposed to be a summer home to complement their regular palatial home at Suffolk and Elm Streets. (From the collection of the Holyoke Public Library.)

Mr. Taft was a renowned world traveler and collector of fine art. The interior reflected those memories of travel to Italy and Austria. Oil paintings, marble statues, rare carpets from the Orient, and even knights in armor were the furnishings here. He had it all until his paper mill failed in 1896. He then sold his Suffolk Street house and moved to the Kenilworth Castle. Unfortunately, he died only one week after moving in. (From the archives of the Holyoke Water Power Company.)

Taft's daughter Lucretia married William Flagg, and together the couple lived at Kenilworth. Mr Flagg was active in local affairs and spoke at civic functions quite frequently. The mansion grew so famous around the world that mail addressed simply to "Mr. Flagg, Kenilworth, Massachusetts," reached its destination. (From the collection of the author.)

Mr. Flagg died first and Lucretia lived on with her servants, becoming more of a recluse by avoiding the unwanted tourists, until her death in 1957. The furnishings were auctioned to antique dealers, but some of the artifacts went to the Yankee Pedlar, the Log Cabin, and some lucky local folks. The house itself was bought by HWP, and they tried to make the building their headquarters, but found it to be structurally unsound. It was then torn down in 1959. Today, a condo complex is situated here. (From the collection of the Holyoke Public Library.)

Five

People and Transportation

This underwater dive team at the dam means its time to inspect the timbers. This view from 1885 shows a barge moored at the face of the dam and two hardy souls ready to dive into the murky water. This was one of the more hazardous jobs in an era without workmen's compensation insurance. (From the archives of the Holyoke Water Power Company.)

This was the club for Holyoke's other movers and shakers. These folks were not invited to join the very prestigious Holyoke Club, so they formed the Other Club, simply a "who's who" in the late 1890s. (From the archives of the Holyoke Water Power Company.)

Going from the business elite to the working class, we now meet the janitor of the HWP, *c.* 1890. Though well dressed, he was working on polishing the railing just before the photographer came along. (From the archives of the Holyoke Water Power Company.)

Block and tackle, jib cranes, and strong men in caps holding steel bars are at work on the wooden dam. They are standing on the part that is normally underwater. This image is from 1885, and they are fixing a defect that the previously seen underwater team has discovered. (From the archives of the Holyoke Water Power Company.)

MURRAY WARD. 6-11   JOHN HOULIHAN 20-0   MAURICE FITZGERALD 14-0   JOHN FITZGERALD FOREMAN   WH. O'CONNOR 14-0   JOHN MYERS 6-6   MICHAEL FITZGERALD 22-0

These seven gentlemen are the maintenance team of the HWP in the early 1920s. (From the archives of the Holyoke Water Power Company.)

On November 5, 1927, at 10:00 am, there was 13.90 feet of water going over the dam, which was almost 5 feet over flood stage. A sandbag crew is seen here trying to save the canal system from being overwhelmed by unregulated water entering at the gatehouse. (From the archives of the Holyoke Water Power Company.)

This is a company group photo of the Holyoke Envelope Company. It is certainly pre-1920. Note the dog on the man's lap in the front row. (From the collection at the Holyoke Heritage State Park.)

From the perspective of touching the most lives, William Stiles Loomis was probably the most important person in Holyoke's history. After returning from the Civil War, Loomis and his brother-in-law bought his father's store. In 1872, he acquired an interest in the *Holyoke Transcript* and became the sole owner in 1875. He sold it to William Dwight in 1887, and Dwight's heirs ran it until it closed in 1993.

In the meantime, Loomis bought a large tract of land, but before he could build houses and otherwise develop it, he needed to provide transportation to the business district. Holyoke Street Railway (HSR) did not want to expand all the way out the business district. So he bought the HSR, expanded their route, and electrified the system to boot. Loomis then developed Brown's farm into what became known as Elmwood. In 1893, the HSR, under Loomis, bought most of Mt. Tom. In 1894, the HSR built Mountain Park, providing trolleys there as well. In 1896, Loomis built the Mt. Tom Railroad and a year later, the Summit House. He helped build the library and Forestdale Cemetery, and he was also the prime mover behind the first old-age home in Holyoke, which later became the Loomis House. William Stiles Loomis was a consummate philanthropist and capitalist. Holyoke was much better for having known him. (From the collection of the Holyoke Public Library.)

In the early years of this century, the Farr Alpaca Company was one of the largest employers in town. A manufacturer of worsted goods and textiles, they were known as a good place to work. Here the company band is helping to celebrate the fiftieth anniversary of the organization. (From the collection at the Holyoke Heritage State Park.)

In 1919, these young women who represented Farr Alpaca in a basketball league are seen looking serious with their headbands, sneakers, and bloomers. (From the collection at the Holyoke Heritage State Park.)

The William Skinner family, seen here around 1885, became very important to the area. The father, William, built the premier silk mill that put Holyoke on the map. The son pictured on the right is Joseph A, who built the Orchards house in South Hadley. Part of those grounds became the Orchards Golf Course. Later, he purchased the summit of Mt. Holyoke with the express purpose of donating it to the state for use as a park. The youngest girl is Katharine, who was the last to live in Wistariahurst and deeded it to the City for a museum. In the front row on the far left is Belle, the person who remodeled the house into the grand place it is today. (From Wistariahurst Museum.)

Belle Skinner is the person responsible for redecorating and enlarging Wistariahurst in the late 1920s. She was a charitable woman who was also known for her work in post-WW I France to reconstruct a town devastated by indiscriminate bombing. (From Wistariahurst Museum.)

At the turn of the century, if you were a young man, there was no better job than that of the newsboy. Here a group is gathered outside the *Holyoke Transcript* on High Street. EXTRA!! EXTRA !! READ ALL ABOUT IT!! (From the collection of the author.)

If you were not as lucky as the newsboys, you could still dream of selling the papers. Seen on Lyman and Front Streets around 1895, these two boys are killing time. (From the archives at the Holyoke Water Power Company.)

In 1953, Emily and Jenny's Restaurant was the place to be if you were a teenager. However, Bob Berrena's favorite customer was his son Bob Jr., the toddler nearest the jukebox. (From the collection of the Berrena family.)

H.P. Hood's workers from the Holyoke creamery are seen here in 1952 enjoying a night-out with their wives at the elegant Roger Smith Hotel on Suffolk Street. (From the collection of the Flatley family.)

This image is of Railroad Street in 1956. The large building just beyond the old freight transfer depot is the Skinner Satin Mill, which was still a large employer. Whiting Coal was the king of coal in town, and just beyond the left edge was where the old passenger station of the New Haven Railroad was located until 1934, when it was torn down. Today this area is the grounds of Holyoke Heritage State Park, the Children's Museum, and the Carousel. (From the collection of the Highland Hardware and Bike Shop.)

The Connecticut River Railroad in the 1880s recognized that Holyoke needed a larger and more impressive passenger station. So they contracted with H.H. Richardson to construct one on Mosher Street, in a stone Romanesque Revival motif. Richardson would later build similar stations on the Boston & Albany Railroad. He would be remembered as one of the country's best designers of impressive railroad stations. This structure still stands and is owned by Perry's Auto Parts. (From the collection of John Doherty.)

This was a largely forgotten station in Holyoke. Riverside Station was located on the B & M at Cabot Street near the Willimansett Bridge. The train in the background is the on the curved bridge over the canal near National Blank Book Company. Until very recently, a small non-descript sign reading, "Riverside" marked this area for the train crews of today. This view is from about 1920. (From the collection of the Holyoke Water Power Company.)

The crowd is gathered at Mt. Tom Junction Station to look at the ice jam in the Connecticut River in March 1936. That ice jam, when it finally let go, damaged the top of the dam. The old station here in later years was converted to other uses. I remember it in the 1970s as the Early Times Lounge. (From the collection of the Holyoke Water Power Company.)

In May 1930, a Boston & Maine Railroad freight train glides north along the sweep of the river just above the dam. This area was the site of big sawmill operations in the 1880s. In the early years of the twentieth century, it was a landfill, as seen here. Today, this scene is viewable from the Mueller Bridge, and it is a lush, green area filled with birds of all types. (From the archives of the Holyoke Water Power Company.)

Seen in 1936, a small Boston & Maine Railroad switching locomotive quietly simmers while awaiting orders at the extensive trackage that used to be near the National Blank Book Company. (From the archives at Holyoke Water Power Company.)

In 1869, the Holyoke & Westfield Railroad was built by the town of Holyoke to provide local shippers an alternative to the exorbitant rates charged by the Connecticut River Railroad. The new line ran to Westfield, where it connected with the New Haven Railroad's Canal Line Division and the nearby Boston & Albany Railroad. This 1880s view is where Holyoke Heritage State Park stands today with the familiar city hall in the background. (From the collection of John Doherty.)

A view to the other direction of the same yard shows the main railroad line back to Westfield. It is interesting to note that the line is operated today by the Pioneer Valley Railroad, which still strongly markets the concept of having a competitive alternative to the other railroad in town. (From the collection of John Doherty.)

A forgotten job of long ago was the one of the gateman. Usually semi-retired or disabled, he would sit in the shack and await a train. At the appropriate time, he would manually lower the gates to stop traffic while the train was nearby. Here at Lyman Street in 1890, he would see about thirty trains a day. (From the collection of John Doherty.)

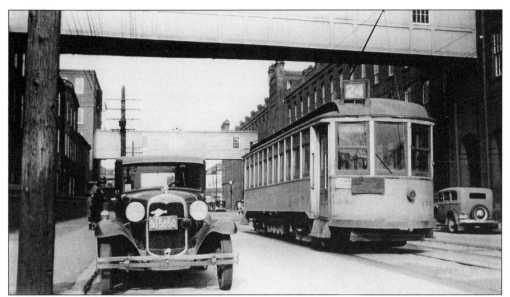

Main Street, a few feet north of Jackson Street, is where we see a Springfield Street Railway trolley in the early 1930s. It is passing under the catwalks at American Thread that allowed for the inter-plant transfer of material. Most recently this site was known as the Elco Dress Company. Just beyond the picture to the right is Clark's Department Store. (From the collection of the Holyoke Public Library.)

This view from the Chicopee side of the Willimansett Bridge shows an "extra" heading into Chicopee. "Extra" means a train that was unscheduled, as noted by the white flags. This photograph was taken early one afternoon in the summer of 1937. (From the collection of the Holyoke Public Library.)

The summer of 1937 was the last year of operation for the electrified trolleys of the HSR. With the city hall and the Marble Building for backdrops, downtown Holyoke was a busy place. (From the collection of the Holyoke Public Library.)

Looking south down High Street from the City Hall Plaza in the early 1930s, one would see a large number of trolleys staged and waiting for passengers to make cross-town or inter-community connections. (From the collection of the Holyoke Public Library.)

The last trolley ran in 1937 when car no. 180 returned from Mountain Park, stopped at the city hall, and then without ceremony continued to the car barns (seen here) on Bridge Street. Later most of the rolling stock of the Holyoke Street Railway were burned on the grade to Mountain Park. (From the collection of the Holyoke Public Library.)

This interesting scene of Main and Mosher Streets from 1957 is still much intact and readily observed today. The gas station, though, is now an auto body shop. (From the archives of the Holyoke Water Power Company.)

On May 3, 1934, a brand-new Gulf service station opened on Lincoln Street. It featured three service bays and a nattily attired attendant, as seen here filling the Chrysler Airflow. Note that Lincoln Street still had the trolley tracks, though there was only three years left of such service. The Super Stop & Shop complex is located today just to the left of this picture. (From the archives of the Holyoke Water Power Company.)

Six

Mountain Park
and Mt. Tom

This sunset drawing (c. 1899) of the layout of the mountain is from a brochure produced by the Holyoke Street Railway (HSR). It shows the pride and joy of the company: Mountain Park, the Mt. Tom Summit House, Mt. Tom Railroad, as well as the extensive trolley network. The concept of the mountaintop resort and the interesting, inclined railway was creative marketing at its best. This was the golden era for trolleys, and many of the owner's of those enterprises were operating resort areas so that they'd have a destination for Saturday and Sunday passengers.

The Delaware Lackawanna & Western Railroad operated a similar such destination park in Sussex County, New Jersey, called Cranberry Lake Park. The park was immensely popular for about only ten years. Then it disappeared as fast as it rose. Mountain Park was in operation until 1987, when it finally closed. (From the collection of the Holyoke Public Library.)

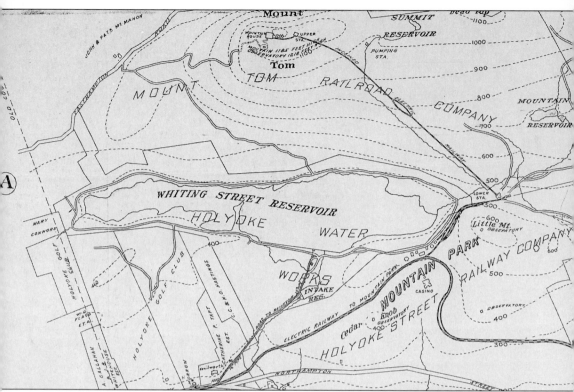

This topographic-type map dates from the 1920s and shows the layout of the Mountain Park and Mt. Tom areas. In the 1880s, the top of Mt. Tom was owned by Mr. Roswell Fairfield, who had bought it to harvest the timber for his Westfield Paper Mill. At the time, his wife Ella was quoted as calling him a fool for purchasing it. Later when he sold it to W.S. Loomis, president of the Holyoke Street Railway, she said, "There are now two fools in Holyoke." (From the collection of the Holyoke Public Library.)

The Collins family bought the park from the HSR in 1952. They ran it successfully until the end in 1987. When I was growing up in Holyoke, I remember this billboard with the clown on the top. As you drove up Northampton Street and saw this sign, it meant the journey was nearly over. Shortly, you would be in the exciting place called Mountain Park. I remember the man on stilts as well, though I don't recall seeing him at the billboard on Route 5. (From the collection of the Holyoke Public Library.)

This image from about 1897 shows a layout of the park at that time. A large crowd has gathered to listen to a concert on the stage, and a few trolleys are parked in the background near the Carousel building. What looks to be a roller coaster is actually the long-forgotten water ride that was a big draw. (From the collection of the Holyoke Public Library.)

Four gents and a dog are seen relaxing on a Sunday in 1897. The freshly laid right-of-way for the town's trolley line is clearly visible, as is the box camera. (From the collection of the Wistariahurst Museum.)

This drawing is from a small pamphlet published by the Holyoke Street Railway that describes the whole Mt. Tom and Mountain Park experience. This picture shows the lower station of the Mt. Tom Railroad with a full car of patrons departing for the summit. The three cars on the right are summer trolleys from downtown Holyoke, discharging passengers at the lower station. (From the author's collection.)

The 1930s saw many summer day-trips sponsored by local businesses to benefit the children of Holyoke. Here, Yeorg's Garage on Chestnut Street has sponsored today's outing. In the last years of Mountain Park's operations, there was talk of having outdoor concerts. There was even preliminary talks of having the Newport Jazz Festival relocate here. However, the Board of Aldermen vetoed that idea right from the start and instead later offered the site to a foreign developer for an off-track betting tele-theater. Luckily, that idea crashed. Presently, at the time of this writing, there are many in town who dream of a multi-million dollar casino complex being sited here. (From the Wistariahurst Museum.)

Here in the 1940s, the trolley passenger discharge area has been converted into a bus turn-around. The famed Mt. Park Ballroom is seen here, and in the background is the roller coaster which was the main attraction. (From the Wistariahurst Museum.)

A view from a few years later shows the facade of the Mt. Park Ballroom slightly changed. This was a major stop for the big-name bands of every era, such as Rudy Vallee, Lawrence Welk, Guy Lombardo, Dion, Gene Pitney, Roy Orbison, The Beach Boys, Sam the Sham and the Pharaohs, etc. They all played the ballroom, which held two thousand fans, and on the weekends, it was always filled to capacity. (From the collection of the Holyoke Public Library.)

In the 1920s, on a hot summer day, there was nothing better than the frozen custard at Mountain Park. (From the Wistariahurst Museum.)

One of the more popular rides of the 1920s–1930s was the Aeroplane ride, which featured the latest in biplane design. Note the long line and the knickers on the boys, who are probably looking for a way to cut that line. (From the Wistariahurst Museum.)

During the 1950s, there was a greater effort on the part of the Mountain Park management to highlight rides made especially for youngsters. The price was reduced for children's level rides to 5¢ each, or six rides for 25¢. (From the Flatley collection.)

Every day, each ride was tested by the employees to ensure the safety of the public. Here, the Wildcat Roller Coaster is on the first run of the day with only one passenger, the ride operator. (From the Wistariahurst Museum.)

When the end came in 1987, most of the rides were sold to other parks around the continent. For example the small diesel train, as well as the 56-foot high ferris wheel, went to Prince Edward Island. The 1929 Wildcat Roller Coaster, seen here when new, went to Iowa where the track and cars provided parts for a similar ride. (From the collection of the Holyoke Public Library.)

The Casino at Mountain Park was a regional theater that attracted many of the Broadway plays from New York City. It was staffed with professional actors and was operated from 1941 to 1963, when the curtain came down for the last time. Some of the famous names to grace the marquee were Hal Holbrook, Peggy Cass, Arlene Francis, Cesar Romero, Merv Griffin, and Tab Hunter. It was torn down in 1972. (From the collection of the Holyoke Public Library.)

What everyone remembers the most about Mountain Park is the carousel. Both children and adults enjoyed the inner-horses that jumped up-and-down, the outer-horses that were stationary, the enchanting music of the calliope, and of course the brass ring that every one tried to get. (From the collection of the Holyoke Public Library.)

This is a 1930s view of the original Carousel building. A similar one stands today at Heritage State Park in downtown Holyoke. In 1987, when Mountain Park closed, the antique carousel ride was valued at $1 million, and the ride was in danger of leaving the area. The Collins family sold it to the city for the discounted price of $850,000; volunteers throughout the community raised the money. And the painted ponies still go 'round and 'round. (From the Wistariahurst Museum.)

This is the cover of a small pamphlet that was produced during the time of second Summit House. It describes the restaurant, the view from the mountain, and the unforgettable trip up there by way of the Mt. Tom Railroad. This brochure and the hundreds of other items that were originally sold in the gift shop of the Summit House are highly valued by collectors. (From the collection at the Holyoke Heritage State Park.)

This view shows a couple at the lower station house at Mountain Park, where passengers boarded the cars for the trip up the steep grade. In 1897, when William Loomis built the Mt. Tom Railroad, he and a friend walked the entire proposed right-of-way to inspect it, and they actually put in a curve rather than destroy a tree. (From the collection of the Wistariahurst Museum.)

An unusual turnout arrangement was employed to allow the two cars to safely pass one another. One car counterweighs the other car which is connected by the thick cable. This site was the first in the nation to employ both a counterweighted system and a passing track on such a steep grade. (From the collection of the Holyoke Public Library.)

On the mountain railway, there were two cars: the Elizur Holyoke and the Rowland Thomas, named of course for the two explorers who had the twin mountains in the area named for them. The steepness of the grade (up to 20%) necessitated slanted seating arrangements. Each car counter-weighted the other, and when one car was at the top, the other was at the bottom. They met in the middle of the ten minute, 1-mile journey. (From the collection of the Wistariahurst Museum.)

Here is the Elizur Holyoke going through the biggest rock-cut on the line in about 1910. In 1946, a B-17 Army Air Corps. bomber, carrying twenty-five airmen on a flight that was supposed to end at Westover, crashed on Mt. Tom. It hit at about the 800-foot high mark and skidded into this cut on the right-of-way. In 1996, Norm Cote and other volunteers organized an effort to place a marker on the site and to plant twenty-five birch trees for the twenty-five dead airmen. (From the collection of the Holyoke Public Library.)

Here the Rowland Thomas car is ascending the grade just above the passing track area with a full complement of passengers who are obviously enjoying the summer morning. This c. 1910 view clearly shows the Elizur Holyoke car below and descending. (From the collection of the Wistariahurst Museum.)

This image from around 1905 shows some tourists exiting the Upper Station and walking along the boardwalk to the Summit House. It was a grand morning in the sun that day overlooking Easthampton. (From the collection of the Wistariahurst Museum.)

In June of 1899, President and Mrs. McKinley arrived at the first Summit House as guests of William Loomis. Looking dapper in his cape and her in a shawl, they are seen here on the promenade boardwalk enjoying the surroundings. They were actually in town to attend the graduation of President McKinley's niece from nearby Mt. Holyoke College. Loomis had a special elite trolley, the Rockrimmon, brought out to be the VIP vehicle for his guests when they arrived at the Boston & Maine Railroad Station in Holyoke. On October 8, 1900, the Summit House burned down. This was a big tourist draw for HSR, so Loomis rebuilt the landmark and the second Summit House opened on May 15, 1901. (From the collection of the Holyoke Public Library.)

The second Summit House was built in time for the 1901 season, and it was much more ornate than the previous one. With its gold-domed top to complement its yellow color, the structure was the landmark of the valley for years. This view, taken in the 1920s, shows just how impressive it really was. The building burned in May of 1929 in a dramatic fire, visible for 50 miles, that was etched into the memories of all the people in the valley. (From the collection of the Highland Hardware and Bike Shop.)

The Dining Room at the Summit House was truly an elegant affair. With its linen tablecloths and ivy-covered walls to add to the view, this was a place of high living. (Postcard from the collection of John Doherty.)

An interesting piece of equipment used at the second Summit House was this workcar. The Mt. Tom Railroad's Upper Station was a few hundred feet from the Summit House, so HSR constructed a short track to allow this electric-powered flatcar to transport food supplies to the restaurant's kitchen. This workcar survived until the very end in 1937 when it was burned to get the metal for recycling. (From the collection of the Holyoke Public Library.)

This is the third Summit House, which was hastily constructed right after the fire of 1929. By this time, though, the high-water mark of mountaintop resorts was past, and the HSR elected to build this smaller and more Spartan version. It was closed down a few years later in 1937, and this was the end of the Mt. Tom Railroad as well. (From the collection of the Highland Hardware and Bike Shop.)

Young Ray D'Addario was aboard this aircraft in 1938 to record the demolition of the third Summit House. Most of the corrugated steel siding was thrown over the side of the mountain where much of it still remains today. The salable steel was brought down and eventually made its way to Japan. This site is occupied today by broadcast television and radio towers. The walkway and its memorable view are still there for the enjoyment of hikers who tour the Monadnock-Metacomet Trail. (From the collection of the Holyoke Public Library.)

About the same season as above, Ray D'Addario took this haunting photograph of the Elizur Holyoke car in the Upper Station awaiting the arrival of the scrapper's torch. Such destruction of history would probably not be allowed to take place today. Mr. D'Addario would later eyewitness and chronicle more unforgettable history as the photographer for the Allies at the Nuremberg War Crimes Tribunals. After which, he came home and opened a camera store on Maple Street in his hometown of Holyoke. This is a man who has seen it all. (From the collection of the Holyoke Public Library.)

Seven
Public Buildings, Places, and Parks

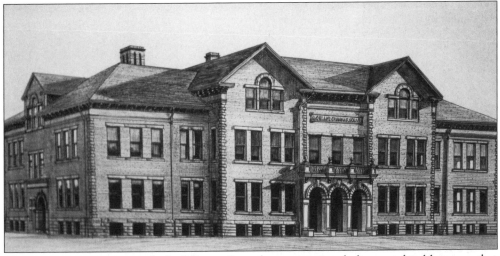

The next nine images are a little different from the conventional photographic likenesses that have been seen thus far. These are actually photos of pen and ink drawings done by John Olsen. Mr. Olsen, a Holyoke native and graduate of the University of Massachusetts, did a series of these highly detailed works for the Holyoke's Centennial Celebration in 1973. They were purchased by the Holyoke Public Library a few years later and were most recently seen en masse as an exhibit in the library's Holyoke History Room in February 1997. The first drawing is the Highland Grammar School, built in 1902 and demolished during the winter of 1997. Interestingly, a time capsule was recovered from the site and is part of the permanent collection of the Library.

The Elmwood School was located on South Street and holds a special memory for me as a place where my friends and I gathered during the summers of 1966–67. Also during those years, the school was used by the Holyoke Community College. Built in 1894, it was demolished in 1980.

The old Ward 1 School was built in 1894 and stood on North Bridge and Dwight Streets. It was demolished in 1916 to make room for the Immaculate Conception School.

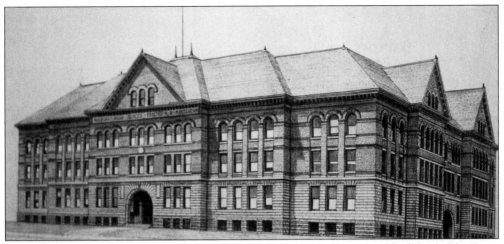

The old Holyoke High School was built in 1898, and located on the block bound by Pine, Sargeant, Beech, and Hampshire Streets. Designed by noted local architect George P.B. Alderman, it burned in a spectacular fire in 1968. I was a student at the new Holyoke High at the time, and the fire was visible from my classes. The companion annex building was demolished in April of 1997.

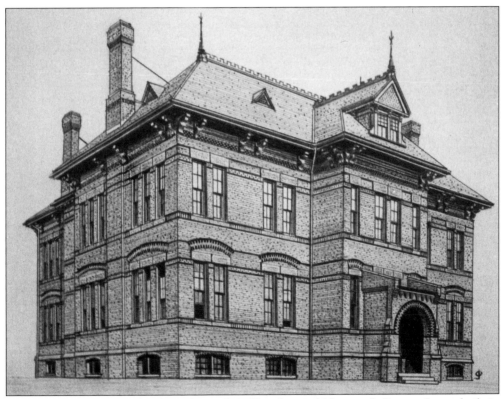

The Nonotuck Street School was located on Hamden and Nonotuck Streets. It was built in 1883 and was demolished in 1956. An apartment building now stands on the site.

The Kirtland School was built in 1900 and served the Oakdale neighborhood from its upper Sargeant Street location until it was closed in 1990 and torn down in March 1997. On February 16, 1997, a reunion banquet was held for the friends and graduates of Kirtland School. Over four hundred people of all ages turned out for an enjoyable evening of reminiscing.

Mt. Tom Hose House was Holyoke's first fire station, built in 1849 and located on Lyman and Canal Streets. It was demolished in 1886 when the current building, also a fire station, was constructed. The site today is occupied by the Pioneer Surface Cleaning Company and is next door to the Holyoke Water Power Company.

The old YMCA building was built in 1892 on the corner of High and Appleton Streets. This was one of the premier locations in the business district and served quite a few businessmen, in addition to the usual complement of school children. It burned down in 1943, and the replacement, which still stands, was built a few blocks further up on Appleton Street.

This is the old South Holyoke Engine House, built on Main Street near Sargeant Street in 1892. This station was the first-response site for most of the large fires that Holyoke was infamous for in the 1970s. The firehouse is still in operation today and appears pretty much the same as it does in the drawing.

Construction was started on the Holyoke City Hall in 1873, the year the city was incorporated, and the building was completed by 1876. Located on High and Dwight Streets, it is a classic rendition of the early English Gothic style. It was designed by C.B. Atwood of Boston, with some later improvements by H.F. Kilburn of New York. The massive tower is 225 feet tall, and the clock face is 8 feet in diameter. This structure once housed the city library, as well as the other city offices, and it was built at a cost of $400,000, a huge amount of money at that time. (From the collection of the Holyoke Public Library.)

In 1897, the Holyoke Water Power Company donated a city block of land which was being used as a ballpark for Holyoke's semi-professional baseball team, the Dudes. A major community fund-raiser was held to obtain the $95,000 needed to build a new library. The finished result, the new Holyoke Public Library, is seen in this view from about 1905, only three years after it was finally built. (From the collection of the Holyoke Public Library.)

This is a photograph of the Mt. Tom Hose House taken c. 1885, shortly before this fire station was torn down to make room for a more modern facility (see the drawing on page 116). (From the archives of the Holyoke Water Power Company.)

This photograph is from the same era, c. 1885, and it shows the old South Holyoke Engine House. Once again, this is a comparison of the Olsen drawing of the same structure on page 117. One can truly appreciate his work by viewing the subject. (From the collection of the Holyoke Public Library.)

A horse and carriage graces the entrance of the old Holyoke Hospital here in the 1870s. The gravel driveway leads to Beech Street, and the building on the left still stands today among the modern complex. (From the collection of the Holyoke Public Library.)

Back in the 1800s, there was a common belief that the air above the smog-ridden cities had a healing, or at least a healthy effect. Don't forget that mountaintop resorts were the rage, and they were advertised as "being of healthy air." This building was constructed on top of a prominent hill in Holyoke so the patients inside could benefit from the altitude. This was the Tuberculosis Hospital, and it stood until the early 1950s on the hill above Cherry Street where the present Soldiers Home is situated. (From the archives of Holyoke Water Power Company.)

This memorial is at Veteran's Park, which is adjacent to the Maple Street Fire Headquarters. It is dedicated to the veterans of the Civil War and contains the names of soldiers from Holyoke who died in that conflict. It features three bas-reliefs of scenes from the war. Ironically, Mr. H.G. Ellicott, a Confederate soldier, was the designer/sculptor. (From the collection at the Holyoke Heritage State Park.)

Tower at Scott Park, Anniversary Hill, Holyoke, Mass.

This is a postcard view of the Scott Tower. This structure and the numerous trails in the adjoining woods were built as part of the WPA projects of the 1930s during the Depression. The tower is still there and affords a grand view of the city in most directions. There is an effort in the neighborhood to rehabilitate the network of trails and stone bridges so that they can be fully enjoyed again. (From the collection of the Holyoke Public Library.)

Holyoke, like most small cities, had numerous movie houses. The ones I remember were the Strand on Maple Street and the Victory on Suffolk Street. There was at least one other one on Main Street; it was called the Majestic Theater. In this view from the 1930s, the Majestic Theater's marquee has a couple of forgettable features. (From the collection of the Holyoke Public Library.)

This picture dates from about 1890, when the place was called Prospect Park. An earlier name was Kerry Park, in honor of the county in Ireland which was the home to many of the folks in the neighborhood. The sign on the leaning pole reads, "No Room for Loafers." The structure along the river is the original Holyoke Canoe Club. (From the collection at Holyoke Heritage State Park.)

This view of the same area as above taken about twenty-five years later shows that the trees have grown significantly, a safety fence has been placed in front of the benches, and the signal poles for the railroad have been moved to the right-of-way. (From the collection of the Holyoke Public Library.)

This old advertising print shows the various locations of the Canoe Club. The 1888 and 1890 structures were near the dam and along the railroad tracks. While the last two structures were up in Smith's Ferry. The last one built in 1903 still stands today. (From the collection at the Holyoke Heritage State Park.)

This view of the third Canoe Club was taken from the South Hadley side of the river in the summer of 1908. It was finished in 1898 at a cost of $3,500 and burned to the ground on March 22, 1909, after the fourth one was finished. Clearly visible beyond are the Kenilworth Castle and the Mt. Tom Summit House. Note the canoeist in the foreground with the straw hat. (From the collection of the Holyoke Public Library.)

Here we are at tea-time on the verandah of the last Canoe Club. Note the beautiful rattan rockers and the interesting details on the lookout tower beyond the folks gathered for this picture. (From the collection of John Doherty.)

The infamous flood of 1936 did a lot of damage to the urban parts of Holyoke. Probably forgotten is the damage done to the Canoe Club. There was so much silt deposited into the basement that it was left there, except for the path shoveled to reach service areas. This photograph was taken on March 21, 1936, at 2:00 pm. (From the archives of the Holyoke Water Power Company.)

This 1950s view shows the shady respite afforded recreationalists launching their boats at the Canoe Club, which by this time was mostly powerboats. The Holyoke Canoe Club today is a family-oriented, affordable retreat that has extensive tennis facilities, as well as boating. (From the archives of the Holyoke Water Power Company.)

In 1960, the Holyoke Water Power Company dedicated a "new" small park along Canal Street that featured extensive plantings, a turbine or water wheel, and the lovely fountains. Among those present at the ceremony were Mayor Samuel Resnic (far right), William Skinner (second from the right), and Robert Barrett (third from the right), who was the president of the Holyoke Water Power Company. (From the archives of the Holyoke Water Power Company.)

Not many people realize that there was an "old" park along Canal Street that was a smaller scale version of what is there today. This 1905 view shows the same general view as the previous photograph, but only one fountain is in place and limited amenities. Note the setting with the old-style railroad grade crossing markers' angles on the embankment and compare with the previous picture. (From the archives of the Holyoke Water Power Company.)

This early 1960s view shows the park being utilized by some of the neighborhood's mill workers, who are enjoying a game of horseshoes on a sunny summer day. (From the archives of the Holyoke Water Power Company.)

Acknowledgments

A book of this sort is never the work of just one person. A number of special people stand out in my mind and without them it would not have been possible. They are listed here in no particular order.

Sandy Christiforidis of the Wistariahurst Museum was supportive from the start of this project and was a great help.

Paul Graves of the Holyoke Museum at the Holyoke Public Library is simply an oracle of information about Holyoke. He has provided much of the color in the text and spent many hours helping me on this project.

The Craven family of the Highland Hardware & Bike Shop kindly allowed me to use some of the beautiful pictures that hang on the walls of their store.

Joanne Lucas and Tom Foley of the Holyoke Water Power Company were gracious enough to open the archives.

Marlene Curran and Charlie Lotspeich of the Holyoke Heritage State Park also were extremely helpful in opening their archives for me. The city is lucky to have them as ambassadors showing the industrial heritage of Holyoke.

John Doherty, a collector of Mt. Tom & Mountain Park memorabilia, was a fountain of information about the times that surrounded the Summit Houses.

Ben Marcus and his staff at Marcus Printing were always cordial and helpful in my needs

Richard Berrena was very generous in allowing me to take pictures of his family off his wall to put into this book.

Pat Woods of the John Woods Realty Company, a stalwart of the community, took a special interest in this project and graciously let me use some of his family's treasured pictures.

I want to especially thank my lovely bride, Kathleen Griffin Della Penna, who was extremely helpful and supportive in this undertaking, as well as the other writing/research projects.